This book belongs to

....

Address

....

....

....

Telephone/Fax

....

A

Name ....

Address...

....

....

.............................Post Code.........................

Telephone...

Name ....

Address...

....

....

.............................Post Code.........................

Telephone...

Name ....

Address...

....

....

.............................Post Code.........................

Telephone...

Name ....

Address...

....

....

.............................Post Code.........................

Telephone...

Name ....

Address...

....

....

.............................Post Code.........................

Telephone...

Name ....

Address...

....

....

.............................Post Code.........................

Telephone...

Name ....

Address...

....

....

.............................Post Code.........................

Telephone...

Name ....

Address...

....

....

.............................Post Code.........................

Telephone...

A

Name ....
Address...
....
....
.............................Post Code.........................
Telephone...

Name ....
Address...
....
....
.............................Post Code.........................
Telephone...

Name ....
Address...
....
....
.............................Post Code.........................
Telephone...

Name ....
Address...
....
....
.............................Post Code.........................
Telephone...

Name ....
Address...
....
....
.............................Post Code.........................
Telephone...

Name ....
Address...
....
....
.............................Post Code.........................
Telephone...

Name ....
Address...
....
....
.............................Post Code.........................
Telephone...

Name ....
Address...
....
....
.............................Post Code.........................
Telephone...

A

Name ....

Address...

....

....

.........................*Post Code*.............................

Telephone...

Name ....

Address...

....

....

.........................*Post Code*.............................

Telephone...

Name ....

Address...

....

....

.........................*Post Code*.............................

Telephone...

Name ....

Address...

....

....

.........................*Post Code*.............................

Telephone...

Name ....

Address...

....

....

.........................*Post Code*.............................

Telephone...

Name ....

Address...

....

....

.........................*Post Code*.............................

Telephone...

Name ....

Address...

....

....

.........................*Post Code*.............................

Telephone...

Name ....

Address...

....

....

.........................*Post Code*.............................

Telephone...

B

Name ....

Address ....

....

....

...........................*Post Code*....................

Telephone ....

Name ....

Address ....

....

....

...........................*Post Code*....................

Telephone ....

Name ....

Address ....

....

....

...........................*Post Code*....................

Telephone ....

Name ....

Address ....

....

....

...........................*Post Code*....................

Telephone ....

Name ....

Address ....

....

....

...........................*Post Code*....................

Telephone ....

Name ....

Address ....

....

....

...........................*Post Code*....................

Telephone ....

Name ....

Address ....

....

....

...........................*Post Code*....................

Telephone ....

Name ....

Address ....

....

....

...........................*Post Code*....................

Telephone ....

B

Name ....
Address...
....
....
.........................Post Code.......................
Telephone...

Name ....
Address...
....
....
.........................Post Code.......................
Telephone...

Name ....
Address...
....
....
.........................Post Code.......................
Telephone...

Name ....
Address...
....
....
.........................Post Code.......................
Telephone...

Name ....
Address...
....
....
.........................Post Code.......................
Telephone...

Name ....
Address...
....
....
.........................Post Code.......................
Telephone...

Name ....
Address...
....
....
.........................Post Code.......................
Telephone...

Name ....
Address...
....
....
.........................Post Code.......................
Telephone...

B

Name ....

Address...

....

....

.................................*Post Code*........................

Telephone...

Name ....

Address...

....

....

.................................*Post Code*........................

Telephone...

Name ....

Address...

....

....

.................................*Post Code*........................

Telephone...

Name ....

Address...

....

....

.................................*Post Code*........................

Telephone...

Name ....

Address...

....

....

.................................*Post Code*........................

Telephone...

Name ....

Address...

....

....

.................................*Post Code*........................

Telephone...

Name ....

Address...

....

....

.................................*Post Code*........................

Telephone...

Name ....

Address...

....

....

.................................*Post Code*........................

Telephone...

C

Name ....

Address...

....

....

...................*Post Code*.......................

Telephone..

Name ....

Address...

....

....

...................*Post Code*.......................

Telephone..

Name ....

Address...

....

....

...................*Post Code*.......................

Telephone..

Name ....

Address...

....

....

...................*Post Code*.......................

Telephone..

Name ....

Address...

....

....

...................*Post Code*.......................

Telephone..

Name ....

Address...

....

....

...................*Post Code*.......................

Telephone..

Name ....

Address...

....

....

...................*Post Code*.......................

Telephone..

Name ....

Address...

....

....

...................*Post Code*.......................

Telephone..

C

Name ....
Address..
....
....
.......................*Post Code*........................
Telephone..

Name ....
Address..
....
....
.......................*Post Code*........................
Telephone..

Name ....
Address..
....
....
.......................*Post Code*........................
Telephone..

Name ....
Address..
....
....
.......................*Post Code*........................
Telephone..

Name ....
Address..
....
....
.......................*Post Code*........................
Telephone..

Name ....
Address..
....
....
.......................*Post Code*........................
Telephone..

Name ....
Address..
....
....
.......................*Post Code*........................
Telephone..

Name ....
Address..
....
....
.......................*Post Code*........................
Telephone..

C

Name ....

Address...

....

....

.............................*Post Code*..........................

Telephone...

Name ....

Address...

....

....

.............................*Post Code*..........................

Telephone...

Name ....

Address...

....

....

.............................*Post Code*..........................

Telephone...

Name ....

Address...

....

....

.............................*Post Code*..........................

Telephone...

Name ....

Address...

....

....

.............................*Post Code*..........................

Telephone...

Name ....

Address...

....

....

.............................*Post Code*..........................

Telephone...

Name ....

Address...

....

....

.............................*Post Code*..........................

Telephone...

Name ....

Address...

....

....

.............................*Post Code*..........................

Telephone...

D

Name ....

Address...

....

....

.............................Post Code.........................

Telephone..

Name ....

Address...

....

....

.............................Post Code.........................

Telephone..

Name ....

Address...

....

....

.............................Post Code.........................

Telephone..

Name ....

Address...

....

....

.............................Post Code.........................

Telephone..

Name ....

Address...

....

....

.............................Post Code.........................

Telephone..

Name ....

Address...

....

....

.............................Post Code.........................

Telephone..

Name ....

Address...

....

....

.............................Post Code.........................

Telephone..

Name ....

Address...

....

....

.............................Post Code.........................

Telephone..

D

Name ....

Address..

....

....

.............................Post Code................................

Telephone..

Name ....

Address..

....

....

.............................Post Code................................

Telephone..

Name ....

Address..

....

....

.............................Post Code................................

Telephone..

Name ....

Address..

....

....

.............................Post Code................................

Telephone..

Name ....

Address..

....

....

.............................Post Code................................

Telephone..

Name ....

Address..

....

....

.............................Post Code................................

Telephone..

Name ....

Address..

....

....

.............................Post Code................................

Telephone..

Name ....

Address..

....

....

.............................Post Code................................

Telephone..

D

Name ....

Address..

....

....

......................*Post Code*......................

Telephone...

Name ....

Address..

....

....

......................*Post Code*......................

Telephone...

Name ....

Address..

....

....

......................*Post Code*......................

Telephone...

Name ....

Address..

....

....

......................*Post Code*......................

Telephone...

Name ....

Address..

....

....

......................*Post Code*......................

Telephone...

Name ....

Address..

....

....

......................*Post Code*......................

Telephone...

Name ....

Address..

....

....

......................*Post Code*......................

Telephone...

Name ....

Address..

....

....

......................*Post Code*......................

Telephone...

E

Name ....
Address...
....
....
.......................Post Code.......................
Telephone...

Name ....
Address...
....
....
.......................Post Code.......................
Telephone...

Name ....
Address...
....
....
.......................Post Code.......................
Telephone...

Name ....
Address...
....
....
.......................Post Code.......................
Telephone...

Name ....
Address...
....
....
.......................Post Code.......................
Telephone...

Name ....
Address...
....
....
.......................Post Code.......................
Telephone...

Name ....
Address...
....
....
.......................Post Code.......................
Telephone...

Name ....
Address...
....
....
.......................Post Code.......................
Telephone...

E

Name	Name ....
Address...	Address...
....	....
....	....
...........................Post Code.........................	...........................Post Code.........................
Telephone...	Telephone...
Name	Name ....
Address...	Address...
....	....
....	....
...........................Post Code.........................	...........................Post Code.........................
Telephone...	Telephone...
Name	Name ....
Address...	Address...
....	....
....	....
...........................Post Code.........................	...........................Post Code.........................
Telephone...	Telephone...
Name	Name ....
Address...	Address...
....	....
....	....
...........................Post Code.........................	...........................Post Code.........................
Telephone...	Telephone...

E

Name ....
Address..
....
....
........................*Post Code*........................
Telephone..

Name ....
Address..
....
....
........................*Post Code*........................
Telephone..

Name ....
Address..
....
....
........................*Post Code*........................
Telephone..

Name ....
Address..
....
....
........................*Post Code*........................
Telephone..

Name ....
Address..
....
....
........................*Post Code*........................
Telephone..

Name ....
Address..
....
....
........................*Post Code*........................
Telephone..

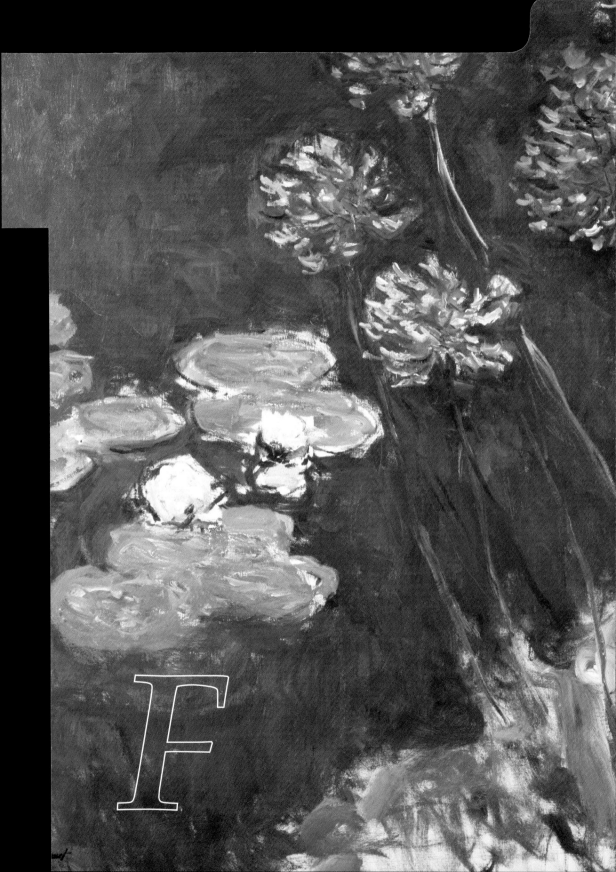

F

Name ....

Address..

....

....

...........................*Post Code*.......................

Telephone..

Name ....

Address..

....

....

...........................*Post Code*.......................

Telephone..

Name ....

Address..

....

....

...........................*Post Code*.......................

Telephone..

Name ....

Address..

....

....

...........................*Post Code*.......................

Telephone..

Name ....

Address..

....

....

...........................*Post Code*.......................

Telephone..

Name ....

Address..

....

....

...........................*Post Code*.......................

Telephone..

Name ....

Address..

....

....

...........................*Post Code*.......................

Telephone..

F

F

Name ....
Address...
....
....
...............................Post Code...................
Telephone...

Name ....
Address...
....
....
...............................Post Code...................
Telephone...

Name ....
Address...
....
....
...............................Post Code...................
Telephone...

Name ....
Address...
....
....
...............................Post Code...................
Telephone...

Name ....
Address...
....
....
...............................Post Code...................
Telephone...

Name ....
Address...
....
....
...............................Post Code...................
Telephone...

Name ....
Address...
....
....
...............................Post Code...................
Telephone...

Name ....
Address...
....
....
...............................Post Code...................
Telephone...

Name ....

Address...

....

....

.............................*Post Code*......................

Telephone...

Name ....

Address...

....

....

.............................*Post Code*......................

Telephone...

Name ....

Address...

....

....

.............................*Post Code*......................

Telephone...

Name ....

Address...

....

....

.............................*Post Code*......................

Telephone...

Name ....

Address...

....

....

.............................*Post Code*......................

Telephone...

Name ....

Address...

....

....

.............................*Post Code*......................

Telephone...

Name ....

Address...

....

....

.............................*Post Code*......................

Telephone...

Name ....

Address...

....

....

.............................*Post Code*......................

Telephone...

F

Name ....

Address..

....

....

.............................*Post Code*........................

Telephone...

Name ....

Address..

....

....

.............................*Post Code*........................

Telephone...

Name ....

Address..

....

....

.............................*Post Code*........................

Telephone...

Name ....

Address..

....

....

.............................*Post Code*........................

Telephone...

Name ....

Address..

....

....

.............................*Post Code*........................

Telephone...

Name ....

Address..

....

....

.............................*Post Code*........................

Telephone...

G

Name ....

Address..

....

....

.............................*Post Code*........................

Telephone...

Name ....

Address..

....

....

.............................*Post Code*........................

Telephone...

G

Name ....
Address...
....
....
...........................*Post Code*.....................
Telephone..

Name ....
Address...
....
....
...........................*Post Code*.....................
Telephone..

Name ....
Address...
....
....
...........................*Post Code*.....................
Telephone..

Name ....
Address...
....
....
...........................*Post Code*.....................
Telephone..

Name ....
Address...
....
....
...........................*Post Code*.....................
Telephone..

Name ....
Address...
....
....
...........................*Post Code*.....................
Telephone..

Name ....
Address...
....
....
...........................*Post Code*.....................
Telephone..

Name ....
Address...
....
....
...........................*Post Code*.....................
Telephone..

G

Name ....

Address..

....

....

............................*Post Code*............................

Telephone..

Name ....

Address..

....

....

............................*Post Code*............................

Telephone..

Name ....

Address..

....

....

............................*Post Code*............................

Telephone..

Name ....

Address..

....

....

............................*Post Code*............................

Telephone..

Name ....

Address..

....

....

............................*Post Code*............................

Telephone..

Name ....

Address..

....

....

............................*Post Code*............................

Telephone..

Name ....

Address..

....

....

............................*Post Code*............................

Telephone..

Name ....

Address..

....

....

............................*Post Code*............................

Telephone..

Name ....

Address...

....

....

...........................*Post Code*...........................

Telephone...

Name ....

Address...

....

....

...........................*Post Code*...........................

Telephone...

Name ....

Address...

....

....

...........................*Post Code*...........................

Telephone...

Name ....

Address...

....

....

...........................*Post Code*...........................

Telephone...

Name ....

Address...

....

....

...........................*Post Code*...........................

Telephone...

Name ....

Address...

....

....

...........................*Post Code*...........................

Telephone...

Name ....

Address...

....

....

...........................*Post Code*...........................

Telephone...

H

H

Name ....
Address..
....
....
...............................Post Code...........................
Telephone...

Name ....
Address..
....
....
...............................Post Code...........................
Telephone...

Name ....
Address..
....
....
...............................Post Code...........................
Telephone...

Name ....
Address..
....
....
...............................Post Code...........................
Telephone...

Name ....
Address..
....
....
...............................Post Code...........................
Telephone...

Name ....
Address..
....
....
...............................Post Code...........................
Telephone...

Name ....
Address..
....
....
...............................Post Code...........................
Telephone...

Name ....
Address..
....
....
...............................Post Code...........................
Telephone...

Name ....

Address..

....

....

...........................*Post Code*........................

Telephone..

Name ....

Address..

....

....

...........................*Post Code*........................

Telephone..

Name ....

Address..

....

....

...........................*Post Code*........................

Telephone..

Name ....

Address..

....

....

...........................*Post Code*........................

Telephone..

Name ....

Address..

....

....

...........................*Post Code*........................

Telephone..

Name ....

Address..

....

....

...........................*Post Code*........................

Telephone..

Name ....

Address..

....

....

...........................*Post Code*........................

Telephone..

Name ....

Address..

....

....

...........................*Post Code*........................

Telephone..

H

Name ....

Address..

....

....

........................*Post Code*............................

Telephone...

Name ....

Address..

....

....

........................*Post Code*............................

Telephone...

Name ....

Address..

....

....

........................*Post Code*............................

Telephone...

Name ....

Address..

....

....

........................*Post Code*............................

Telephone...

Name ....

Address..

....

....

........................*Post Code*............................

Telephone...

Name ....

Address..

....

....

........................*Post Code*............................

Telephone...

Name ....

Address..

....

....

........................*Post Code*............................

Telephone...

Name ....

Address..

....

....

........................*Post Code*............................

Telephone...

I

I

Name	*Name* ....
Address..	*Address*..
....	....
....	....
........................*Post Code*..................	........................*Post Code*..................
Telephone..	*Telephone*..
Name	*Name* ....
Address..	*Address*..
....	....
....	....
........................*Post Code*..................	........................*Post Code*..................
Telephone..	*Telephone*..
Name	*Name* ....
Address..	*Address*..
....	....
....	....
........................*Post Code*..................	........................*Post Code*..................
Telephone..	*Telephone*..
Name	*Name* ....
Address..	*Address*..
....	....
....	....
........................*Post Code*..................	........................*Post Code*..................
Telephone..	*Telephone*..

Name ....

Address...

....

....

....*Post Code*.........................

Telephone..

Name ....

Address...

....

....

....*Post Code*.........................

Telephone..

Name ....

Address...

....

....

....*Post Code*.........................

Telephone..

Name ....

Address...

....

....

....*Post Code*.........................

Telephone..

Name ....

Address...

....

....

....*Post Code*.........................

Telephone..

Name ....

Address...

....

....

....*Post Code*.........................

Telephone..

Name ....

Address...

....

....

....*Post Code*.........................

Telephone..

Name ....

Address...

....

....

....*Post Code*.........................

Telephone..

I

Name ....

Address...

....

....

...............................*Post Code*............................

Telephone...

Name ....

Address...

....

....

...............................*Post Code*............................

Telephone...

Name ....

Address...

....

....

...............................*Post Code*............................

Telephone...

Name ....

Address...

....

....

...............................*Post Code*............................

Telephone...

Name ....

Address...

....

....

...............................*Post Code*............................

Telephone...

Name ....

Address...

....

....

...............................*Post Code*............................

Telephone...

Name ....

Address...

....

....

...............................*Post Code*............................

Telephone...

Name ....

Address...

....

....

...............................*Post Code*............................

Telephone...

J

J

Name ....

Address..

....

....

.........................Post Code.......................

Telephone...

Name ....

Address..

....

....

.........................Post Code.......................

Telephone...

Name ....

Address..

....

....

.........................Post Code.......................

Telephone...

Name ....

Address..

....

....

.........................Post Code.......................

Telephone...

Name ....

Address..

....

....

.........................Post Code.......................

Telephone...

Name ....

Address..

....

....

.........................Post Code.......................

Telephone...

Name ....

Address..

....

....

.........................Post Code.......................

Telephone...

Name ....

Address..

....

....

.........................Post Code.......................

Telephone...

Name ....

Address..

....

....

..............................*Post Code*..........................

Telephone...

Name ....

Address..

....

....

..............................*Post Code*..........................

Telephone...

Name ....

Address..

....

....

..............................*Post Code*..........................

Telephone...

Name ....

Address..

....

....

..............................*Post Code*..........................

Telephone...

Name ....

Address..

....

....

..............................*Post Code*..........................

Telephone...

Name ....

Address..

....

....

..............................*Post Code*..........................

Telephone...

Name ....

Address..

....

....

..............................*Post Code*..........................

Telephone...

Name ....

Address..

....

....

..............................*Post Code*..........................

Telephone...

J

Name ....

Address..

....

....

......................................*Post Code*......................

Telephone..

Name ....

Address..

....

....

......................................*Post Code*......................

Telephone..

Name ....

Address..

....

....

......................................*Post Code*......................

Telephone..

Name ....

Address..

....

....

......................................*Post Code*......................

Telephone..

Name ....

Address..

....

....

......................................*Post Code*......................

Telephone..

Name ....

Address..

....

....

......................................*Post Code*......................

Telephone..

Name ....

Address..

....

....

......................................*Post Code*......................

Telephone..

K

Name ....

Address..

....

....

......................................*Post Code*......................

Telephone..

K

Name ....
Address...
....
....
...........................Post Code.....................
Telephone..

Name ....
Address...
....
....
...........................Post Code.....................
Telephone..

Name ....
Address...
....
....
...........................Post Code.....................
Telephone..

Name ....
Address...
....
....
...........................Post Code.....................
Telephone..

Name ....
Address...
....
....
...........................Post Code.....................
Telephone..

Name ....
Address...
....
....
...........................Post Code.....................
Telephone..

Name ....
Address...
....
....
...........................Post Code.....................
Telephone..

Name ....
Address...
....
....
...........................Post Code.....................
Telephone..

Name ....

Address...

....

....

............................*Post Code*............................

Telephone...

Name ....

Address...

....

....

............................*Post Code*............................

Telephone...

Name ....

Address...

....

....

............................*Post Code*............................

Telephone...

Name ....

Address...

....

....

............................*Post Code*............................

Telephone...

Name ....

Address...

....

....

............................*Post Code*............................

Telephone...

Name ....

Address...

....

....

............................*Post Code*............................

Telephone...

Name ....

Address...

....

....

............................*Post Code*............................

Telephone...

Name ....

Address...

....

....

............................*Post Code*............................

Telephone...

K

Name ....

Address..

....

....

.........................*Post Code*..........................

Telephone..

Name ....

Address..

....

....

.........................*Post Code*..........................

Telephone..

Name ....

Address..

....

....

.........................*Post Code*..........................

Telephone..

Name ....

Address..

....

....

.........................*Post Code*..........................

Telephone..

Name ....

Address..

....

....

.........................*Post Code*..........................

Telephone..

Name ....

Address..

....

....

.........................*Post Code*..........................

Telephone..

Name ....

Address..

....

....

.........................*Post Code*..........................

Telephone..

L

L

Name	Name
Address	Address
Post Code	Post Code
Telephone	Telephone

Name	Name
Address	Address
Post Code	Post Code
Telephone	Telephone

Name	Name
Address	Address
Post Code	Post Code
Telephone	Telephone

Name	Name
Address	Address
Post Code	Post Code
Telephone	Telephone

Name ....

Address..

....

....

....*Post Code*..........................

Telephone...

Name ....

Address..

....

....

....*Post Code*..........................

Telephone...

Name ....

Address..

....

....

....*Post Code*..........................

Telephone...

Name ....

Address..

....

....

....*Post Code*..........................

Telephone...

Name ....

Address..

....

....

....*Post Code*..........................

Telephone...

Name ....

Address..

....

....

....*Post Code*..........................

Telephone...

L

Name ....

Address..

....

....

.................................*Post Code*.........................

Telephone...

Name ....

Address..

....

....

.................................*Post Code*.........................

Telephone...

Name ....

Address..

....

....

.................................*Post Code*.........................

Telephone...

Name ....

Address..

....

....

.................................*Post Code*.........................

Telephone...

Name ....

Address..

....

....

.................................*Post Code*.........................

Telephone...

Name ....

Address..

....

....

.................................*Post Code*.........................

Telephone...

M

Name ....

Address..

....

....

.................................*Post Code*.........................

Telephone...

Name ....

Address..

....

....

.................................*Post Code*.........................

Telephone...

M

Name ....

Address..

....

....

................................Post Code................................

Telephone..

Name ....

Address..

....

....

................................Post Code................................

Telephone..

Name ....

Address..

....

....

................................Post Code................................

Telephone..

Name ....

Address..

....

....

................................Post Code................................

Telephone..

Name ....

Address..

....

....

................................Post Code................................

Telephone..

Name ....

Address..

....

....

................................Post Code................................

Telephone..

Name ....

Address..

....

....

................................Post Code................................

Telephone..

Name ....

Address..

....

....

................................Post Code................................

Telephone..

Name ....

Address..

....

....

..............................*Post Code*...........................

Telephone...

Name ....

Address..

....

....

..............................*Post Code*...........................

Telephone...

Name ....

Address..

....

....

..............................*Post Code*...........................

Telephone...

Name ....

Address..

....

....

..............................*Post Code*...........................

Telephone...

Name ....

Address..

....

....

..............................*Post Code*...........................

Telephone...

Name ....

Address..

....

....

..............................*Post Code*...........................

Telephone...

Name ....

Address..

....

....

..............................*Post Code*...........................

Telephone...

Name ....

Address..

....

....

..............................*Post Code*...........................

Telephone...

M

Name ....

Address..

....

....

............................*Post Code*.........................

Telephone...

Name ....

Address..

....

....

............................*Post Code*.........................

Telephone...

Name ....

Address..

....

....

............................*Post Code*.........................

Telephone...

Name ....

Address..

....

....

............................*Post Code*.........................

Telephone...

Name ....

Address..

....

....

............................*Post Code*.........................

Telephone...

Name ....

Address..

....

....

............................*Post Code*.........................

Telephone...

Name ....

Address..

....

....

............................*Post Code*.........................

Telephone...

Name ....

Address..

....

....

............................*Post Code*.........................

Telephone...

N

N

Name ....

Address...

....

....

...............................Post Code...........................

Telephone...

Name ....

Address...

....

....

...............................Post Code...........................

Telephone...

Name ....

Address...

....

....

...............................Post Code...........................

Telephone...

Name ....

Address...

....

....

...............................Post Code...........................

Telephone...

Name ....

Address...

....

....

...............................Post Code...........................

Telephone...

Name ....

Address...

....

....

...............................Post Code...........................

Telephone...

Name ....

Address...

....

....

...............................Post Code...........................

Telephone...

Name ....

Address...

....

....

...............................Post Code...........................

Telephone...

N

Name ....

Address...

....

....

.........................*Post Code*.......................

Telephone...

Name ....

Address...

....

....

.........................*Post Code*.......................

Telephone...

Name ....

Address...

....

....

.........................*Post Code*.......................

Telephone...

Name ....

Address...

....

....

.........................*Post Code*.......................

Telephone...

Name ....

Address...

....

....

.........................*Post Code*.......................

Telephone...

Name ....

Address...

....

....

.........................*Post Code*.......................

Telephone...

Name ....

Address...

....

....

.........................*Post Code*.......................

Telephone...

Name ....

Address...

....

....

.........................*Post Code*.......................

Telephone...

Name ....

Address...

....

....

...............................*Post Code*.........................

Telephone..

Name ....

Address...

....

....

...............................*Post Code*.........................

Telephone..

Name ....

Address...

....

....

...............................*Post Code*.........................

Telephone..

Name ....

Address...

....

....

...............................*Post Code*.........................

Telephone..

Name ....

Address...

....

....

...............................*Post Code*.........................

Telephone..

Name ....

Address...

....

....

...............................*Post Code*.........................

Telephone..

Name ....

Address...

....

....

...............................*Post Code*.........................

Telephone..

Name ....

Address...

....

....

...............................*Post Code*.........................

Telephone..

O

O

Name ....
Address...
....
....
..........................*Post Code*..........................
Telephone...

Name ....
Address...
....
....
..........................*Post Code*..........................
Telephone...

Name ....
Address...
....
....
..........................*Post Code*..........................
Telephone...

Name ....
Address...
....
....
..........................*Post Code*..........................
Telephone...

Name ....
Address...
....
....
..........................*Post Code*..........................
Telephone...

Name ....
Address...
....
....
..........................*Post Code*..........................
Telephone...

Name ....
Address...
....
....
..........................*Post Code*..........................
Telephone...

Name ....
Address...
....
....
..........................*Post Code*..........................
Telephone...

Name ....

Address..

....

....

..............................*Post Code*......................

Telephone...

Name ....

Address..

....

....

..............................*Post Code*......................

Telephone...

Name ....

Address..

....

....

..............................*Post Code*......................

Telephone...

Name ....

Address..

....

....

..............................*Post Code*......................

Telephone...

Name ....

Address..

....

....

..............................*Post Code*......................

Telephone...

Name ....

Address..

....

....

..............................*Post Code*......................

Telephone...

Name ....

Address..

....

....

..............................*Post Code*......................

Telephone...

Name ....

Address..

....

....

..............................*Post Code*......................

Telephone...

O

Name ....

Address..

....

....

...........................*Post Code*.........................

Telephone...

Name ....

Address..

....

....

...........................*Post Code*.........................

Telephone...

Name ....

Address..

....

....

...........................*Post Code*.........................

Telephone...

Name ....

Address..

....

....

...........................*Post Code*.........................

Telephone...

Name ....

Address..

....

....

...........................*Post Code*.........................

Telephone...

Name ....

Address..

....

....

...........................*Post Code*.........................

Telephone...

Name ....

Address..

....

....

...........................*Post Code*.........................

Telephone...

Name ....

Address..

....

....

...........................*Post Code*.........................

Telephone...

P

P

Name	*Name* ....
Address..	*Address*..
....	....
....	....
.......................*Post Code*.................	.......................*Post Code*.................
Telephone..	*Telephone*..
Name	*Name* ....
Address..	*Address*..
....	....
....	....
.......................*Post Code*.................	.......................*Post Code*.................
Telephone..	*Telephone*..
Name	*Name* ....
Address..	*Address*..
....	....
....	....
.......................*Post Code*.................	.......................*Post Code*.................
Telephone..	*Telephone*..
Name	*Name* ....
Address..	*Address*..
....	....
....	....
.......................*Post Code*.................	.......................*Post Code*.................
Telephone..	*Telephone*..

Name ....

Address...

....

....

...................................*Post Code*....................

Telephone..

Name ....

Address...

....

....

...................................*Post Code*....................

Telephone..

Name ....

Address...

....

....

...................................*Post Code*....................

Telephone..

Name ....

Address...

....

....

...................................*Post Code*....................

Telephone..

Name ....

Address...

....

....

...................................*Post Code*....................

Telephone..

Name ....

Address...

....

....

...................................*Post Code*....................

Telephone..

Name ....

Address...

....

....

...................................*Post Code*....................

Telephone..

Name ....

Address...

....

....

...................................*Post Code*....................

Telephone..

P

Name ....

Address..

....

....

...............................*Post Code*.........................

Telephone...

Name ....

Address..

....

....

...............................*Post Code*.........................

Telephone...

Name ....

Address..

....

....

...............................*Post Code*.........................

Telephone...

Name ....

Address..

....

....

...............................*Post Code*.........................

Telephone...

Name ....

Address..

....

....

...............................*Post Code*.........................

Telephone...

Name ....

Address..

....

....

...............................*Post Code*.........................

Telephone...

Name ....

Address..

....

....

...............................*Post Code*.........................

Telephone...

Name ....

Address..

....

....

...............................*Post Code*.........................

Telephone...

Q

Name ....

Address...

....

....

.......................Post Code.........................

Telephone...

Name ....

Address...

....

....

.......................Post Code.........................

Telephone...

Name ....

Address...

....

....

.......................Post Code.........................

Telephone...

Name ....

Address...

....

....

.......................Post Code.........................

Telephone...

Name ....

Address...

....

....

.......................Post Code.........................

Telephone...

Name ....

Address...

....

....

.......................Post Code.........................

Telephone...

Name ....

Address...

....

....

.......................Post Code.........................

Telephone...

Name ....

Address...

....

....

.......................Post Code.........................

Telephone...

Q

Name ....

Address..

....

....

............................*Post Code*............................

Telephone..

Name ....

Address..

....

....

............................*Post Code*............................

Telephone..

Name ....

Address..

....

....

............................*Post Code*............................

Telephone..

Name ....

Address..

....

....

............................*Post Code*............................

Telephone..

Name ....

Address..

....

....

............................*Post Code*............................

Telephone..

Name ....

Address..

....

....

............................*Post Code*............................

Telephone..

Q

Name ....

Address..

....

....

............................*Post Code*............................

Telephone..

Name ....

Address..

....

....

............................*Post Code*............................

Telephone..

Name ....

Address..

....

....

.............................*Post Code*.........................

Telephone..

Name ....

Address..

....

....

.............................*Post Code*.........................

Telephone..

Name ....

Address..

....

....

.............................*Post Code*.........................

Telephone..

Name ....

Address..

....

....

.............................*Post Code*.........................

Telephone..

Name ....

Address..

....

....

.............................*Post Code*.........................

Telephone..

Name ....

Address..

....

....

.............................*Post Code*.........................

Telephone..

Name ....

Address..

....

....

.............................*Post Code*.........................

Telephone..

Name ....

Address..

....

....

.............................*Post Code*.........................

Telephone..

R

R

Name ....

Address...

....

....

.................Post Code.................

Telephone...

Name ....

Address...

....

....

.................Post Code.................

Telephone...

Name ....

Address...

....

....

.................Post Code.................

Telephone...

Name ....

Address...

....

....

.................Post Code.................

Telephone...

Name ....

Address...

....

....

.................Post Code.................

Telephone...

Name ....

Address...

....

....

.................Post Code.................

Telephone...

Name ....

Address...

....

....

.................Post Code.................

Telephone...

Name ....

Address...

....

....

.................Post Code.................

Telephone...

Name ....

Address...

....

....

.......................*Post Code*.........................

Telephone...

Name ....

Address...

....

....

.......................*Post Code*.........................

Telephone...

Name ....

Address...

....

....

.......................*Post Code*.........................

Telephone...

Name ....

Address...

....

....

.......................*Post Code*.........................

Telephone...

Name ....

Address...

....

....

.......................*Post Code*.........................

Telephone...

Name ....

Address...

....

....

.......................*Post Code*.........................

Telephone...

Name ....

Address...

....

....

.......................*Post Code*.........................

Telephone...

Name ....

Address...

....

....

.......................*Post Code*.........................

Telephone...

R

Name ....

Address...

....

....

.............................*Post Code*...........................

Telephone...

Name ....

Address...

....

....

.............................*Post Code*...........................

Telephone...

Name ....

Address...

....

....

.............................*Post Code*...........................

Telephone...

Name ....

Address...

....

....

.............................*Post Code*...........................

Telephone...

Name ....

Address...

....

....

.............................*Post Code*...........................

Telephone...

Name ....

Address...

....

....

.............................*Post Code*...........................

Telephone...

Name ....

Address...

....

....

.............................*Post Code*...........................

Telephone...

Name ....

Address...

....

....

.............................*Post Code*...........................

Telephone...

S

S

Name ....
Address...
....
....
.................................Post Code..................
Telephone...

Name ....
Address...
....
....
.................................Post Code..................
Telephone...

Name ....
Address...
....
....
.................................Post Code..................
Telephone...

Name ....
Address...
....
....
.................................Post Code..................
Telephone...

Name ....
Address...
....
....
.................................Post Code..................
Telephone...

Name ....
Address...
....
....
.................................Post Code..................
Telephone...

Name ....
Address...
....
....
.................................Post Code..................
Telephone...

Name ....
Address...
....
....
.................................Post Code..................
Telephone...

Name ....

Address...

....

....

..............................*Post Code*.........................

Telephone...

Name ....

Address...

....

....

..............................*Post Code*.........................

Telephone...

Name ....

Address...

....

....

..............................*Post Code*.........................

Telephone...

Name ....

Address...

....

....

..............................*Post Code*.........................

Telephone...

Name ....

Address...

....

....

..............................*Post Code*.........................

Telephone...

Name ....

Address...

....

....

..............................*Post Code*.........................

Telephone...

Name ....

Address...

....

....

..............................*Post Code*.........................

Telephone...

Name ....

Address...

....

....

..............................*Post Code*.........................

Telephone...

S

S

Name	*Name* ....
Address...	*Address*...
....	....
....	....
...........................*Post Code*....................	...........................*Post Code*....................
Telephone..	*Telephone*..
Name	*Name* ....
Address...	*Address*...
....	....
....	....
...........................*Post Code*....................	...........................*Post Code*....................
Telephone..	*Telephone*..
Name	*Name* ....
Address...	*Address*...
....	....
....	....
...........................*Post Code*....................	...........................*Post Code*....................
Telephone..	*Telephone*..
Name	*Name* ....
Address...	*Address*...
....	....
....	....
...........................*Post Code*....................	...........................*Post Code*....................
Telephone..	*Telephone*..

Name ....

Address...

....

....

.............................*Post Code*............................

Telephone..

Name ....

Address...

....

....

.............................*Post Code*............................

Telephone..

Name ....

Address...

....

....

.............................*Post Code*............................

Telephone..

Name ....

Address...

....

....

.............................*Post Code*............................

Telephone..

Name ....

Address...

....

....

.............................*Post Code*............................

Telephone..

Name ....

Address...

....

....

.............................*Post Code*............................

Telephone..

Name ....

Address...

....

....

.............................*Post Code*............................

Telephone..

S

Name ....

Address...

....

....

.............................*Post Code*............................

Telephone..

Name ....

Address..

....

....

...............................*Post Code*.........................

Telephone..

Name ....

Address..

....

....

...............................*Post Code*.........................

Telephone..

Name ....

Address..

....

....

...............................*Post Code*.........................

Telephone..

Name ....

Address..

....

....

...............................*Post Code*.........................

Telephone..

Name ....

Address..

....

....

...............................*Post Code*.........................

Telephone..

Name ....

Address..

....

....

...............................*Post Code*.........................

Telephone..

Name ....

Address..

....

....

...............................*Post Code*.........................

Telephone..

T

T

Name ....

Address..

....

....

...........................Post Code.................................

Telephone..

Name ....

Address..

....

....

...........................Post Code.................................

Telephone..

Name ....

Address..

....

....

...........................Post Code.................................

Telephone..

Name ....

Address..

....

....

...........................Post Code.................................

Telephone..

Name ....

Address..

....

....

...........................Post Code.................................

Telephone..

Name ....

Address..

....

....

...........................Post Code.................................

Telephone..

Name ....

Address..

....

....

...........................Post Code.................................

Telephone..

Name ....

Address..

....

....

...........................Post Code.................................

Telephone..

Name ....

Address..

....

....

..............................*Post Code*........................

Telephone...

Name ....

Address..

....

....

..............................*Post Code*........................

Telephone...

Name ....

Address..

....

....

..............................*Post Code*........................

Telephone...

Name ....

Address..

....

....

..............................*Post Code*........................

Telephone...

Name ....

Address..

....

....

..............................*Post Code*........................

Telephone...

Name ....

Address..

....

....

..............................*Post Code*........................

Telephone...

Name ....

Address..

....

....

..............................*Post Code*........................

Telephone...

Name ....

Address..

....

....

..............................*Post Code*........................

Telephone...

T

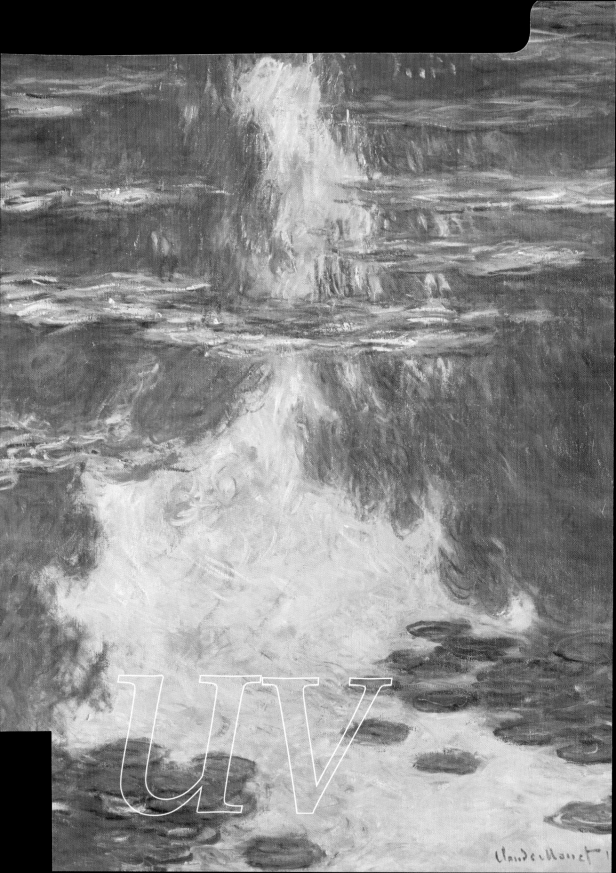

Name ....

Address...

....

....

...............................*Post Code*..........................

Telephone...

Name ....

Address...

....

....

...............................*Post Code*..........................

Telephone...

Name ....

Address...

....

....

...............................*Post Code*..........................

Telephone...

Name ....

Address...

....

....

...............................*Post Code*..........................

Telephone...

Name ....

Address...

....

....

...............................*Post Code*..........................

Telephone...

Name ....

Address...

....

....

...............................*Post Code*..........................

Telephone...

Name ....

Address...

....

....

...............................*Post Code*..........................

Telephone...

Name ....

Address...

....

....

...............................*Post Code*..........................

Telephone...

UV

Name ....

Address...

....

....

...........................*Post Code*.........................

Telephone...

Name ....

Address...

....

....

...........................*Post Code*.........................

Telephone...

Name ....

Address...

....

....

...........................*Post Code*.........................

Telephone...

Name ....

Address...

....

....

...........................*Post Code*.........................

Telephone...

Name ....

Address...

....

....

...........................*Post Code*.........................

Telephone...

Name ....

Address...

....

....

...........................*Post Code*.........................

Telephone...

Name ....

Address...

....

....

...........................*Post Code*.........................

Telephone...

W

Name ....
Address...
....
....
.........................Post Code.........................
Telephone...

Name ....
Address...
....
....
.........................Post Code.........................
Telephone...

Name ....
Address...
....
....
.........................Post Code.........................
Telephone...

Name ....
Address...
....
....
.........................Post Code.........................
Telephone...

Name ....
Address...
....
....
.........................Post Code.........................
Telephone...

Name ....
Address...
....
....
.........................Post Code.........................
Telephone...

Name ....
Address...
....
....
.........................Post Code.........................
Telephone...

Name ....
Address...
....
....
.........................Post Code.........................
Telephone...

W

Name ....

Address..

....

....

................................*Post Code*................................

Telephone..

Name ....

Address..

....

....

................................*Post Code*................................

Telephone..

Name ....

Address..

....

....

................................*Post Code*................................

Telephone..

Name ....

Address..

....

....

................................*Post Code*................................

Telephone..

Name ....

Address..

....

....

................................*Post Code*................................

Telephone..

Name ....

Address..

....

....

................................*Post Code*................................

Telephone..

Name ....

Address..

....

....

................................*Post Code*................................

Telephone..

Name ....

Address..

....

....

................................*Post Code*................................

Telephone..

W

Name ....

Address...

....

....

.............................Post Code..........................

Telephone..

Name ....

Address...

....

....

.............................Post Code..........................

Telephone..

Name ....

Address...

....

....

.............................Post Code..........................

Telephone..

Name ....

Address...

....

....

.............................Post Code..........................

Telephone..

Name ....

Address...

....

....

.............................Post Code..........................

Telephone..

Name ....

Address...

....

....

.............................Post Code..........................

Telephone..

Name ....

Address...

....

....

.............................Post Code..........................

Telephone..

Name ....

Address...

....

....

.............................Post Code..........................

Telephone..

XY

Name ....

Address...

....

....

.................................*Post Code*.........................

Telephone...

Name ....

Address...

....

....

.................................*Post Code*.........................

Telephone...

Name ....

Address...

....

....

.................................*Post Code*.........................

Telephone...

Name ....

Address...

....

....

.................................*Post Code*.........................

Telephone...

Name ....

Address...

....

....

.................................*Post Code*.........................

Telephone...

Name ....

Address...

....

....

.................................*Post Code*.........................

Telephone...

Name ....

Address...

....

....

.................................*Post Code*.........................

Telephone...

Name ....

Address...

....

....

.................................*Post Code*.........................

Telephone...

Z

Birthdays
Anniversaries
and Events

JANUARY

1	*5*	*9*	*13*
2	*6*	*10*	*14*
3	*7*	*11*	*15*
4	*8*	*12*	*16*

JANUARY

17	21	25	29
18	22	26	30
19	23	27	31
20	24	28	

FEBRUARY

1	5	9	13
2	6	10	14
3	7	11	15
4	8	12	16

FEBRUARY

17	21	25	29
18	22	26	
19	23	27	
20	24	28	

MARCH

1	5	9	13
2	6	10	14
3	7	11	15
4	8	12	16

MARCH

17	21	25	29
18	22	26	30
19	23	27	31
20	24	28	

APRIL

1	5	9	13
2	6	10	14
3	7	11	15
4	8	12	16

APRIL

17	*21*	*25*	*29*
18	*22*	*26*	*30*
19	*23*	*27*	
20	*24*	*28*	

MAY

1	5	9	13
2	6	10	14
3	7	11	15
4	8	12	16

MAY

17	21	25	29
18	22	26	30
19	23	27	31
20	24	28	

JUNE

1	5	9	13
2	6	10	14
3	7	11	15
4	8	12	16

JUNE

17	21	25	29
18	22	26	30
19	23	27	
20	24	28	

JULY

1	5	9	13
2	6	10	14
3	7	11	15
4	8	12	16

JULY

17	21	25	29
18	22	26	30
19	23	27	31
20	24	28	

AUGUST

1	5	9	13
2	6	10	14
3	7	11	15
4	8	12	16

AUGUST

17	*21*	*25*	*29*
18	*22*	*26*	*30*
19	*23*	*27*	*31*
20	*24*	*28*	

SEPTEMBER

1	*5*	*9*	*13*
2	*6*	*10*	*14*
3	*7*	*11*	*15*
4	*8*	*12*	*16*

SEPTEMBER

17	21	25	29
18	22	26	30
19	23	27	
20	24	28	

OCTOBER

1	5	9	13
2	6	10	14
3	7	11	15
4	8	12	16

OCTOBER

17	*21*	*25*	*29*
18	*22*	*26*	*30*
19	*23*	*27*	*31*
20	*24*	*28*	

NOVEMBER

1	5	9	13
2	6	10	14
3	7	11	15
4	8	12	16

NOVEMBER

17	21	25	29
18	22	26	30
19	23	27	
20	24	28	

DECEMBER

1	*5*	*9*	*13*
2	*6*	*10*	*14*
3	*7*	*11*	*15*
4	*8*	*12*	*16*

DECEMBER

17	21	25	29
18	22	26	30
19	23	27	31
20	24	28	

Christmas
Card List

Name .... Year ....

Name .... Year ....

Name .... Year ....

Name .... Year ....

Name .... Year ....

Name .... Year ....

Name .... Year ....

Name .... Year ....

Name .... Year ....

Name .... Year ....

Name .... Year ....

Name .... Year ....

Name .... Year ....

Name .... Year ....

Name .... Year ....

Name .... Year ....

Name .... Year ....

Name .... Year ....

Name .... Year ....

Name .... Year ....

Name .... *Year* ....

Name .... *Year* ....

Name .... *Year* ....

Name .... *Year* ....

Name .... *Year* ....

Name .... *Year* ....

Name .... *Year* ....

Name .... *Year* ....

Name .... *Year* ....

Name .... *Year* ....

Name .... *Year* ....

Name .... *Year* ....

Name .... *Year* ....

Name .... *Year* ....

Name .... *Year* ....

Name .... *Year* ....

Name .... *Year* ....

Name .... *Year* ....

Name .... *Year* ....

Name .... *Year* ....

Name .... *Year* ....

Name .... *Year* ....

Name .... *Year* ....

Name .... *Year* ....

Name .... *Year* ....

Name .... *Year* ....

Name .... *Year* ....

Name .... *Year* ....

Name .... *Year* ....

Name .... *Year* ....

Name .... *Year* ....

Name .... *Year* ....

Name .... *Year* ....

Name .... *Year* ....

Name .... *Year* ....

Name .... *Year* ....

Name .... *Year* ....

Name .... *Year* ....

Name .... *Year* ....

Name .... *Year* ....

Name .... Year ....

Name .... Year ....

Name .... Year ....

Name .... Year ....

Name .... Year ....

Name .... Year ....

Name .... Year ....

Name .... Year ....

Name .... Year ....

Name .... Year ....

Name .... Year ....

Name .... Year ....

Name .... Year ....

Name .... Year ....

Name .... Year ....

Name .... Year ....

Name .... Year ....

Name .... Year ....

Name .... Year ....

Name .... Year ....

Name .... Year ....

Name .... Year ....

Name .... Year ....

Name .... Year ....

Name .... Year ....

Name .... Year ....

Name .... Year ....

Name .... Year ....

Name .... Year ....

Name .... Year ....

Name .... Year ....

Name .... Year ....

Name .... Year ....

Name .... Year ....

Name .... Year ....

Name .... Year ....

Name .... Year ....

Name .... Year ....

Name .... Year ....

Name .... Year ....

Name .... Year ....

Name .... Year ....

Name .... Year ....

Name .... Year ....

Name .... Year ....

Name .... Year ....

Name .... Year ....

Name .... Year ....

Name .... Year ....

Name .... Year ....

Name .... Year ....

Name .... Year ....

Name .... Year ....

Name .... Year ....

Name .... Year ....

Name .... Year ....

Name .... Year ....

Name .... Year ....

Name .... Year ....

Name .... Year ....

Name .... *Year* ....

Name .... *Year* ....

Name .... *Year* ....

Name .... *Year* ....

Name .... *Year* ....

Name .... *Year* ....

Name .... *Year* ....

Name .... *Year* ....

Name .... *Year* ....

Name .... *Year* ....

Name .... *Year* ....

Name .... *Year* ....

Name .... *Year* ....

Name .... *Year* ....

Name .... *Year* ....

Name .... *Year* ....

Name .... *Year* ....

Name .... *Year* ....

Name .... *Year* ....

Name .... *Year* ....

Name .... Year ....

Name .... Year ....

Name .... Year ....

Name .... Year ....

Name .... Year ....

Name .... Year ....

Name .... Year ....

Name .... Year ....

Name .... Year ....

Name .... Year ....

Name .... Year ....

Name .... Year ....

Name .... Year ....

Name .... Year ....

Name .... Year ....

Name .... Year ....

Name .... Year ....

Name .... Year ....

Name .... Year ....

Name .... Year ....

Name .... Year ....

Name .... Year ....

Name .... Year ....

Name .... Year ....

Name .... Year ....

Name .... Year ....

Name .... Year ....

Name .... Year ....

Name .... Year ....

Name .... Year ....

Name .... Year ....

Name .... Year ....

Name .... Year ....

Name .... Year ....

Name .... Year ....

Name .... Year ....

Name .... Year ....

Name .... Year ....

Name .... Year ....

Name .... Year ....

Name .... Year ....

Name .... Year ....

Name .... Year ....

Name .... Year ....

Name .... Year ....

Name .... Year ....

Name .... Year ....

Name .... Year ....

Name .... Year ....

Name .... Year ....

Name .... Year ....

Name .... Year ....

Name .... Year ....

Name .... Year ....

Name .... Year ....

Name .... Year ....

Name .... Year ....

Name .... Year ....

Name .... Year ....

Name .... Year ....

Name .... *Year* ....

Name .... *Year* ....

Name .... *Year* ....

Name .... *Year* ....

Name .... *Year* ....

Name .... *Year* ....

Name .... *Year* ....

Name .... *Year* ....

Name .... *Year* ....

Name .... *Year* ....

Name .... *Year* ....

Name .... *Year* ....

Name .... *Year* ....

Name .... *Year* ....

Name .... *Year* ....

Name .... *Year* ....

Name .... *Year* ....

Name .... *Year* ....

Name .... *Year* ....

Name .... *Year* ....

Name .... *Year* ....

Name .... *Year* ....

Name .... *Year* ....

Name .... *Year* ....

Name .... *Year* ....

Name .... *Year* ....

Name .... *Year* ....

Name .... *Year* ....

Name .... *Year* ....

Name .... *Year* ....

Name .... *Year* ....

Name .... *Year* ....

Name .... *Year* ....

Name .... *Year* ....

Name .... *Year* ....

Name .... *Year* ....

Name .... *Year* ....

Name .... *Year* ....

Name .... *Year* ....

Name .... *Year* ....

Name .... *Year* ....

Name .... *Year* ....

Name .... *Year* ....

Name .... *Year* ....

Name .... *Year* ....

Name .... *Year* ....

Name .... *Year* ....

Name .... *Year* ....

Name .... *Year* ....

Name .... *Year* ....

Name .... *Year* ....

Name .... *Year* ....

Name .... *Year* ....

Name .... *Year* ....

Name .... *Year* ....

Name .... *Year* ....

Name .... *Year* ....

Name .... *Year* ....

Name .... *Year* ....

Name .... *Year* ....

Name .... *Year* ....

Name .... *Year* ....

Name .... *Year* ....

Name .... *Year* ....

Name .... *Year* ....

Name .... *Year* ....

Name .... *Year* ....

Name .... *Year* ....

Name .... *Year* ....

Name .... *Year* ....

Name .... *Year* ....

Name .... *Year* ....

Name .... *Year* ....

Name .... *Year* ....

Name .... *Year* ....

Name .... *Year* ....

Name .... *Year* ....

Name .... *Year* ....

Name .... *Year* ....

Name .... *Year* ....

Name .... *Year* ....

Name .... *Year* ....

Name .... *Year* ....

Name .... *Year* ....

Name .... *Year* ....

Name .... *Year* ....

Name .... *Year* ....

Name .... *Year* ....

Name .... *Year* ....

Name .... *Year* ....

Name .... *Year* ....

Name .... *Year* ....

Name .... *Year* ....

Name .... *Year* ....

Name .... *Year* ....

Name .... *Year* ....

Name .... *Year* ....

Name .... *Year* ....

Name .... *Year* ....

Name .... *Year* ....

Name .... *Year* ....

Name .... *Year* ....

Name .... *Year* ....

Name .... *Year* ....

Name .... *Year* ....

Name .... *Year* ....

Name .... *Year* ....

Name .... *Year* ....

Name .... *Year* ....

Name .... *Year* ....

Name .... *Year* ....

Name .... *Year* ....

Name .... *Year* ....

Name .... *Year* ....

Name .... *Year* ....

Name .... *Year* ....

Name .... *Year* ....

Name .... *Year* ....

Name .... *Year* ....

Name .... *Year* ....

Name .... *Year* ....

Name .... *Year* ....

Name .... *Year* ....

Name .... *Year* ....

Name .... *Year* ....

Name .... *Year* ....

Name .... *Year* ....

Name .... *Year* ....

Name .... *Year* ....

Name .... *Year* ....

Name .... *Year* ....

Name .... *Year* ....

Name .... *Year* ....

Name .... *Year* ....

Name .... *Year* ....

Name .... *Year* ....

Name .... *Year* ....

Name .... *Year* ....

Name .... *Year* ....

Name .... *Year* ....

Name .... *Year* ....

Name .... *Year* ....

Name .... *Year* ....

Name .... *Year* ....

Name .... *Year* ....

Name .... *Year* ....

Name .... *Year* ....

Name .... *Year* ....

Name .... *Year* ....

Name .... *Year* ....

Name .... *Year* ....

Name .... *Year* ....

Name .... *Year* ....

Name .... *Year* ....

Name .... *Year* ....

Name .... *Year* ....

Name .... *Year* ....

Name .... *Year* ....

Name .... *Year* ....

Name .... *Year* ....

Name .... *Year* ....

Name .... *Year* ....

*Gifts and
Ideas List*

Name	Occasion	Date
....	....	....
....	....	....
....	....	....
....	....	....
....	....	....
....	....	....
....	....	....
....	....	....
....	....	....
....	....	....
....	....	....
....	....	....
....	....	....
....	....	....
....	....	....
....	....	....
....	....	....

Name	Occasion	Date
....	....	....
....	....	....
....	....	....
....	....	....
....	....	....
....	....	....
....	....	....
....	....	....
....	....	....
....	....	....
....	....	....
....	....	....
....	....	....
....	....	....
....	....	....
....	....	....
....	....	....

Name	Occasion	Date

Name	Occasion	Date
....	....	....
....	....	....
....	....	....
....	....	....
....	....	....
....	....	....
....	....	....
....	....	....
....	....	....
....	....	....
....	....	....
....	....	....
....	....	....
....	....	....
....	....	....
....	....	....
....	....	....

Name	Occasion	Date
....	....	....
....	....	....
....	....	....
....	....	....
....	....	....
....	....	....
....	....	....
....	....	....
....	....	....
....	....	....
....	....	....
....	....	....
....	....	....
....	....	....
....	....	....
....	....	....
....	....	....

Name	Occasion	Date

Name	*Occasion*	*Date*
....	....	....
....	....	....
....	....	....
....	....	....
....	....	....
....	....	....
....	....	....
....	....	....
....	....	....
....	....	....
....	....	....
....	....	....
....	....	....
....	....	....
....	....	....
....	....	....
....	....	....

Name	Occasion	Date
....	....	....
....	....	....
....	....	....
....	....	....
....	....	....
....	....	....
....	....	....
....	....	....
....	....	....
....	....	....
....	....	....
....	....	....
....	....	....
....	....	....
....	....	....
....	....	....
....	....	....
....	....	....

Name	Occasion	Date
....	....	....
....	....	....
....	....	....
....	....	....
....	....	....
....	....	....
....	....	....
....	....	....
....	....	....
....	....	....
....	....	....
....	....	....
....	....	....
....	....	....
....	....	....
....	....	....
....	....	....
....	....	....

Name	*Occasion*	*Date*

Name	Occasion	Date
....	....	....
....	....	....
....	....	....
....	....	....
....	....	....
....	....	....
....	....	....
....	....	....
....	....	....
....	....	....
....	....	....
....	....	....
....	....	....
....	....	....
....	....	....
....	....	....
....	....	....
....	....	....

Name	Occasion	Date

Name	Occasion	Date

Name	Occasion	Date

Name	Occasion	Date
....	....	....
....	....	....
....	....	....
....	....	....
....	....	....
....	....	....
....	....	....
....	....	....
....	....	....
....	....	....
....	....	....
....	....	....
....	....	....
....	....	....
....	....	....
....	....	....
....	....	....

Name	Occasion	Date
....	....	....
....	....	....
....	....	....
....	....	....
....	....	....
....	....	....
....	....	....
....	....	....
....	....	....
....	....	....
....	....	....
....	....	....
....	....	....
....	....	....
....	....	....
....	....	....
....	....	....
....	....	....

Name	Occasion	Date
....	....	....
....	....	....
....	....	....
....	....	....
....	....	....
....	....	....
....	....	....
....	....	....
....	....	....
....	....	....
....	....	....
....	....	....
....	....	....
....	....	....
....	....	....
....	....	....
....	....	....

Name	*Occasion*	*Date*

Name	Occasion	Date

Claude Monet

pictures featured throughout this book:

Cover :

Waterlilies (oil on canvas)
by Claude Monet (1840 -1926)
Private Collection /Bridgeman Art Library

Frontispiece :

White Nenuphars. 1899
by Claude Monet (1840 -1926)
Pushkin Museum, Moscow /Bridgeman Art Library

A Waterlilies (oil on canvas)
by Claude Monet (1840 -1926)
Private Collection /Bridgeman Art Library

B Path through the Poppies, Ile Saint-Martin, Vetheuil, 1880
by Claude Monet (1840 -1926)
Metropolitan Museum of Art, New York /Bridgeman Art Library

C The Artist's Garden at Giverny, 1900 (oil on canvas)
by Claude Monet (1840 -1926)
Musee d'Orsay /Giraudon /Bridgeman Art Library

D Villas in Bordighera, 1884
by Claude Monet (1840 -1926)
Museum of Art, Santa Barbara /Bridgeman Art Library

E The Grand Canal, Venice, c. 1908
by Claude Monet (1840 -1926)
Palace of the Legion of Honor, San Francisco/
Bridgeman Art Library

F Waterlilies and Agapanthus, 1914 -17 (oil on canvas)
by Claude Monet (1840 -1926)
Musee Marmottan /Peter Willi /Bridgeman Art Library

G Villas in Bordighera, 1884
by Claude Monet (1840 -1926)
Museum of Art, Santa Barbara /Bridgeman Art Library

H The Grand Canal, Venice, c. 1908
by Claude Monet (1840 -1926)
Palace of the Legion of Honor, San Francisco/
Bridgeman Art Library

I The Church at Vetheuil, 1880
by Claude Monet (1840 -1926)
Southampton City Art Gallery /Bridgeman Art Library

J White Nenuphars. 1899
by Claude Monet (1840 -1926)
Pushkin Museum, Moscow /Bridgeman Art Library

K Chemin de la Cavee, Pourville, 1882
by Claude Monet (1840 -1926)
Private Collection /Peter Willi /Bridgeman Art Library

L The Bridge at Argenteuil , 1874 (oil on canvas)
by Claude Monet (1840 -1926)
Musee d'Orsay /Giraudon /Bridgeman Art Library

M Blanche Monet Painting
by Claude Monet (1840 -1926)
Los Angeles County Museum of Art /Bridgeman Art Library

N The Waterlily Pond, 1917-19 (oil on canvas)
by Claude Monet (1840 -1926)
Musee Marmottan /Peter Willi /Bridgeman Art Library

O Haystack at Giverny, 1886 (oil on canvas)
by Claude Monet (1840 -1926)
Hermitage, St. Petersburg /Bridgeman Art Library

P The Artist's Garden at Vetheuil, 1880
by Claude Monet (1840 -1926)
National Gallery of Art, Washington DC /Lauros-Giraudon/
Bridgeman Art Library

Q Woman with Parasol turned to the Left, 1886
by Claude Monet (1840 -1926)
Musee d'Orsay /Peter Willi /Bridgeman Art Library

R Antibes, 1888
by Claude Monet (1840 -1926)
Courtauld Gallery, London /Bridgeman Art Library

S Sunflowers, 1881 (oil on canvas)
by Claude Monet (1840 -1926)
Metropolitan Museum of Art, New York/
Bridgeman Art Library

T Haystack at Giverny, 1886 (oil on canvas)
by Claude Monet (1840 -1926)
Hermitage, St. Petersburg /Bridgeman Art Library

UV Waterlilies, 1907 (oil on canvas)
by Claude Monet (1840 -1926)
Private Collection /Bridgeman Art Library

W Blanche Monet Painting
by Claude Monet (1840 -1926)
Los Angeles County Museum of Art /Bridgeman Art Library

XY The Bridge at Argenteuil , 1874 (oil on canvas)
by Claude Monet (1840 -1926)
Musee d'Orsay /Giraudon /Bridgeman Art Library

Z Antibes, View of the Cap, Mistral Wind, 1888 (oil on canvas)
by Claude Monet (1840 -1926)
Private Collection / Christie's Images /Bridgeman Art Library

Birthdays, Anniversaries & Events
The Bridge at Argenteuil , 1874 (oil on canvas)
by Claude Monet (1840 -1926)
Musee d'Orsay /Giraudon /Bridgeman Art Library

Christmas Card List
The Magpie, 1869 (oil on canvas)
by Claude Monet (1840 -1926)
Musee d'Orsay /Peter Willi /Bridgeman Art Library

Gifts & Ideas List
The Artist's Garden at Giverny, 1900 (oil on canvas)
by Claude Monet (1840 -1926)
Musee d'Orsay /Giraudon /Bridgeman Art Library